WHAT MAKES YOU ILL?

Mike Unwin & Kate Woodward

Designed by Non Figg
Illustrated by Annabel Spenceley and Kuo Kang Chen

Editor: Susan Meredith

Consultant: Dr Kevan Thorley

CONTENTS

Additional designs by Lindy Dark

All about being ill

Most of the time you probably feel well. Your body can do lots of things without you even thinking about them.

Your brain lets you think clearly.

Most of the time you are happy and feel comfortable inside.

Your skin looks smooth and healthy.

You feel energetic and want to run around and play.

Your arms and legs feel strong.

You get hungry if you have not eaten for a while.

Ill or well?

You can usually tell if you are ill because things feel wrong with your body. These things are called symptoms. You can often tell what is wrong by the kind of symptoms you have.

You may feel hot one minute, then cold the next.

Your tummy may feel shaky and you may need to be sick.

You might feel tired and achy and want to lie down.

You feel miserable, and do not want to join in your friends' games.

You might have a pain somewhere.

You may lose your appetite.

What is pain?

Having a pain is one way your body tells you something is wrong.

Sometimes you can easily see what is wrong because of where it hurts.

Sometimes you have a pain in one place when really the problem is somewhere else. Tonsillitis causes a tummy ache, even though your tonsils are in your throat.

Getting better

Your body is good at getting better by itself. You can help it mend by resting. There are lots of ways to keep busy while you rest.

Watching TV

Reading

Playing games

Listening to music

Plenty of love and attention from your family or friends can make you feel better too.

If resting doesn't help, and you don't get better on your own, you may have to visit your doctor.

Keeping well

Looking after yourself helps you stay well. Eating the right food and exercising keep you fit. Being fit helps you fight illness and get better more quickly if you are ill.

Sports and energetic games keep you fit.

Fruit is a healthy food to eat.

Why do you get ill?

People become ill for many different reasons. Most everyday illnesses are caused by germs. Your body usually fights germs off but sometimes they make you ill. This is called having an infection.

There are many different kinds of germ. They cause different symptoms of infection.

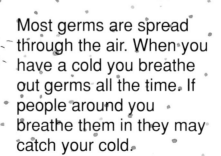

Tummy ache

Sore throat

Headache

Rash

Sneezing sprays millions of germs into the air.

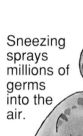

Most germs are spread through the air. When you have a cold you breathe out germs all the time. If people around you breathe them in they may catch your cold.

Where you live

Where you live can affect your health. For example, traffic fumes and factory smoke can pollute the air you breathe. This can make people ill.

Accidents

Sometimes accidents can hurt you or make you ill. Many accidents happen at home.

Falling can give you cuts or bruises or even break your bones.

Hot things can burn you. Always be careful with hot food.

Feelings

Your feelings can make you ill too. Worrying may upset your tummy and make you feel sick.

Feeling nervous about your first day at a new school can make you feel ill.

Family illnesses

Some illnesses tend to run in families. Scientists now know someone is more likely to get asthma if one of their parents has it. Asthma makes it difficult to breathe properly.

People with asthma can take medicine to help them run around and play sports.

Allergies

Ordinary things like cat hair, pollen from plants, and certain foods make some people feel poorly. This is called having an allergy.

An allergy to strawberries can give you a rash.

5

What is a germ?

Germs are tiny, living things. They are everywhere: in the air you breathe, on your skin, in your food and on the things you touch.

The three main kinds of germs are called bacteria, viruses and fungi.

Germs are so tiny you need a microscope to see them.

There are germs inside your body all the time. Most of them don't do you any harm. Some can even be helpful, but others make you ill.

Some useful bacteria live in your tummy. They help you to digest your food.

Bacteria

Bacteria are so tiny that over a thousand could fit on a pinhead. Some can cause illnesses such as ear and skin infections.

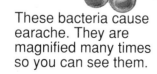

These bacteria cause earache. They are magnified many times so you can see them.

Viruses

Viruses are over a million times smaller than bacteria. They cause many common infections such as colds, tummy upsets and sore throats.

This kind of virus causes sore throats.

If you look at viruses through very strong microscopes, you can see their strange shapes.

Keeping germs out

Your body is built to keep harmful germs out as much as possible. This picture shows how your body protects you.

Eyelashes stop dirt and germs from getting into your eyes.

You have tears in your eyes all the time. They help wash out germs.

Tiny hairs in your nose catch germs you breathe in.

Your skin keeps germs out as long as you have no cuts or scratches.

Germs come out of your nose in slimy stuff called mucus, when you sneeze or blow your nose.

Your mouth and throat are always wet and slippery so that germs don't get stuck there.

Tongue

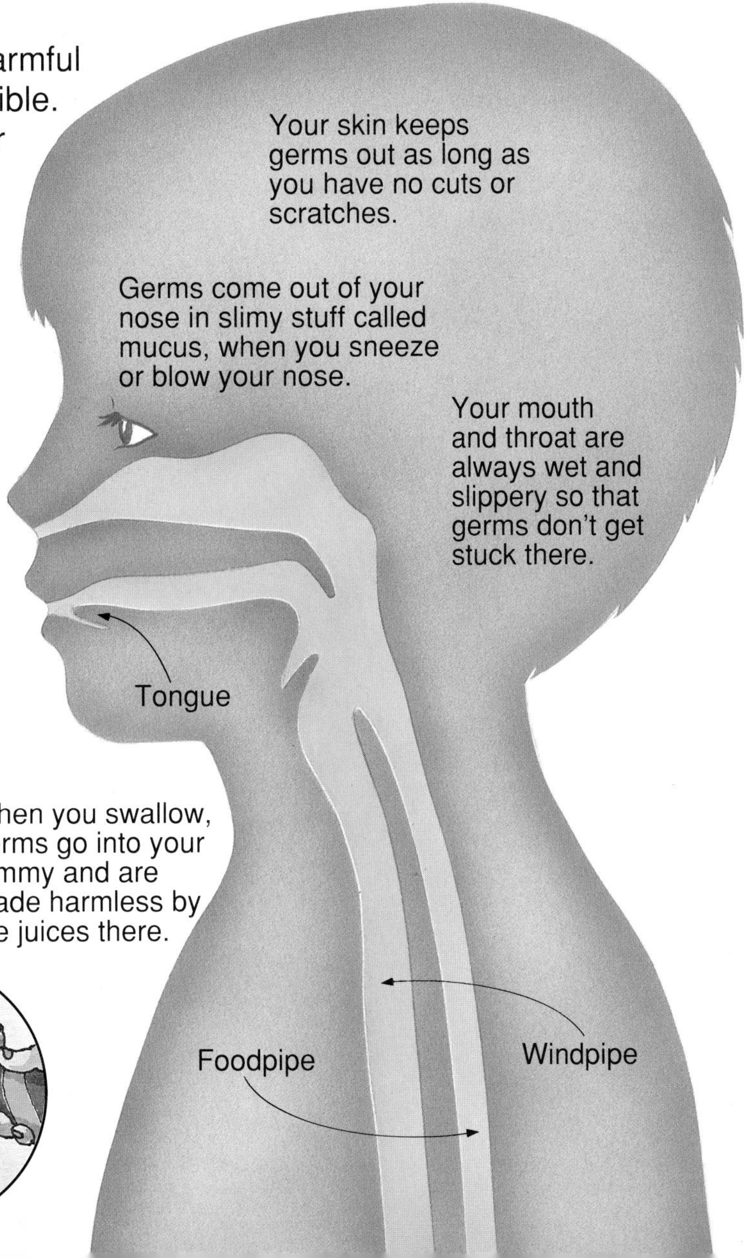

Fungi

These are germs which grow on your body and cause infections. Athlete's foot is a fungus which can grow between your toes. It makes your skin look sore and flaky.

You can get rid of athlete's foot with special powder.

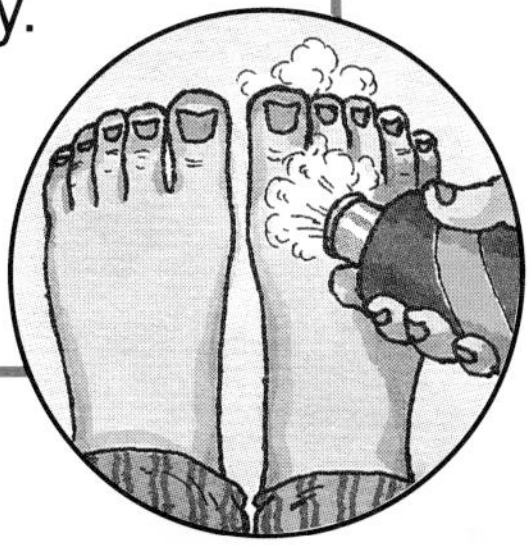

When you swallow, germs go into your tummy and are made harmless by the juices there.

Foodpipe

Windpipe

Germ attack

Your whole body is made up of millions of tiny living parts called cells. When germs such as bacteria or viruses get into your body they start to multiply and feed off your cells. This makes you feel ill.

Bacteria invasion

Your body is a warm, damp place with plenty of food, so bacteria grow and spread quickly inside you. Within hours there can be millions in one small part of your body.

This is what cells from your skin look like through a very strong microscope.

Some bacteria attack your cells by giving off poisons. These can also spread infection around your body in your blood.

Cell

Poisons

Bacteria

Bacteria attack cell with poisons.

Virus invasion

Viruses attack by getting inside a cell. The cell becomes a kind of factory for making new viruses.

Virus enters cell.

New viruses are made inside cell.

Cells die and viruses set out to invade new cells.

Germs and symptoms

Symptoms are caused both by germs damaging your cells, and by the way your body fights back. Different germs cause symptoms in different parts of your body.

An area infected by bacteria, such as an aching tooth, often feels sore and swollen.

Your temperature rises as your body starts to fight the germs. This is an early sign of infection.

Colds and flu often start with a sore throat because the viruses that cause them start in your throat.

Cleaning cuts and protecting them with a plaster or bandage helps to stop bacteria from getting in.

A medicine called paracetamol helps lower your temperature.

In the blood

Your blood is always flowing inside you. It takes food and oxygen around your body. But it can also help spread any infections that get into your blood.

Getting better

Medicines called antibiotics can help treat illnesses caused by bacteria. No medicines can get rid of viruses. Your body fights them in its own way.

Fighting back

When you get an infection your body fights off the invading germs. In your blood there are special cells to try and stop them from spreading further.

The germ eaters

When germs damage your cells, more blood flows to the infected place. White blood cells then devour the germs.

Germ

1. White blood cell sticks to germs.

2. White blood cell surrounds germs.

3. Germs are digested inside.

In your blood

This page shows a close-up picture of blood vessels. These are the tubes that carry blood around your body. Blood contains millions of cells in a liquid called plasma. Red blood cells carry food and oxygen. White blood cells have the job of killing germs.

Plasma

White blood cell

Red blood cell

Flushing out germs

Lymph is a liquid that runs around your body in a network of tubes. It carries dead germs and cells to swellings called lymph nodes. Here, white blood cells clean them out of the lymph.

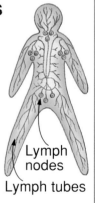

Lymph nodes

Lymph tubes

Lymph nodes, especially in your neck, can feel sore and swollen while you are fighting germs.

Permanent protection

During an infection, special white blood cells called lymphocytes kill germs using chemicals known as antibodies.

Antibody

1. Antibodies hold onto germ.

2. Germ bursts open and dies.

Germ

Antibodies can recognize germs that have attacked you before. They stay in your body to stop the same germs from attacking again. This means you only catch most infections once. Being protected like this is called being immune.

Immunization

Immunization is a way of making you immune to an infectious illness without your ever having to catch it.

When you are immunized, you are given a tiny dose of a germ. The dose is too weak to make you ill, but it helps your body produce the antibodies that will protect you against that illness in the future.

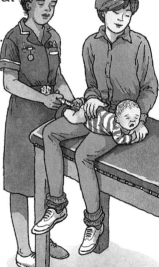

Babies are usually given injections that immunize them against some serious illnesses.

11

Allergies

An allergy is when your body fights ordinary things as if they were germs. This can cause symptoms such as a rash, wheezing or tummy ache. Anything that causes an allergy in somebody is called an allergen.

What happens

When an allergen invades the body of an allergic person, white blood cells send out antibodies to fight it. A chemical called histamine is produced, which causes the allergic symptoms.

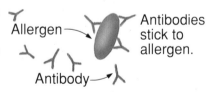

Allergen

Antibody

Antibodies stick to allergen.

Histamine

White blood cell

White blood cell produces histamine.

Breathing

Some people are allergic to things they breathe in, such as dust, pollen, feathers or pet hairs.

Hay fever can be caused by an allergy to pollen. It makes you sneeze and your eyes become watery and itchy.

What is asthma?

Asthma can be caused by an allergy. It makes it difficult to breathe air into your lungs, so you wheeze or cough. Here you can see what happens.

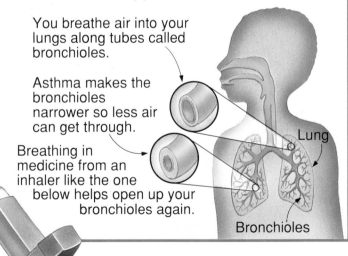

You breathe air into your lungs along tubes called bronchioles.

Asthma makes the bronchioles narrower so less air can get through.

Breathing in medicine from an inhaler like the one below helps open up your bronchioles again.

Lung

Bronchioles

12

Touching

Some people have to be careful what they wear against their skin. Metal, for instance in earrings, and material such as wool, can cause a rash.

An itchy rash called eczema is sometimes caused by washing powder or soap.

Metal

Wool

Eating

Some people are allergic to certain foods. Eating them can cause allergic symptoms including a tummy ache or rash. Food allergy can play a part in asthma.

These foods can cause allergies in some people.

Milk

Seafood

Chocolate

Treating allergies

You cannot catch allergies from other people. The best protection against them is for people to try to avoid things they know they are allergic to.

It is hard to avoid allergens such as dust which get everywhere. People allergic to dust need their bedrooms cleaned or dusted regularly.

Medicines called antihistamines can ease some of the symptoms caused by allergies.

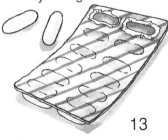

13

How illnesses spread

The most common way that illnesses are spread is through the air. When you cough, sneeze or breathe out, you spray tiny droplets into the air. This can spread illnesses such as colds, flu and chickenpox to other people.

Covering your mouth and nose when you cough or sneeze helps stop germs from spreading. One sneeze can shoot germs over three metres (10 feet).

Touching

Some skin infections, such as cold sores or warts, can be spread from one person to another by touching the infected place.

Try not to share other people's things, such as towels or unwashed dishes and cutlery, if they have an infection.

Food

If you do not take enough care with food, germs can make it bad and cause illness. Bacteria grow on fresh food such as meat and milk if it is kept for too long.

Fresh food should always be washed before cooking or eating.

Food lasts longer if it is kept somewhere cold.

A cover protects food from flies, which can carry bacteria.

14

Washing hands

Always wash your hands after going to the toilet, and before eating or handling food. Dirty hands can spread germs onto food and cause bad upset tummies.

Soil can occasionally carry a serious disease caused by dog or cat mess, so take care to wash your hands after playing outside in parks or gardens.

Occasionally some pets can pass on diseases. It is always best to wash your hands after handling animals, and not to kiss them, or let them lick your face.

Headlice

Headlice are tiny creatures that can live in your hair and make your head feel itchy. Lice and their eggs (called nits) can get from one person's head to another's.

Tie long hair back for school, and don't share brushes or combs.

Bad water

Water can also carry diseases. This sometimes happens in poorer places where people have to share the same dirty water for washing, drinking and cooking.

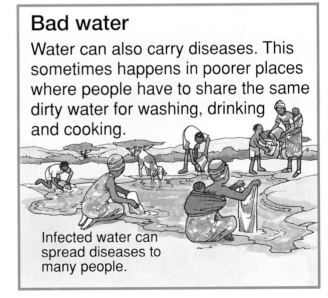

Infected water can spread diseases to many people.

Accidents

If ever you get hurt or injured, whether it is a tiny cut or a broken leg, your body has its own ways of mending itself.

Cuts and grazes

If your skin is broken by a cut or graze and your blood vessels are damaged, blood flows out of your body. Tiny blood cells called platelets soon stop the bleeding by making a sticky plug called a clot.

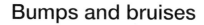

Bumps and bruises

A hard bump can damage blood vessels without breaking your skin. Blood leaks out underneath your skin, but it cannot escape. This causes a bruise.

Chemicals from red blood cells can make bruises look purple.

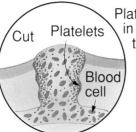

Platelets clump together in the blood around the cut.

Cut   Platelets

Blood cell

The platelets catch other blood cells and make a clot.

Clot

New skin cells

Blood cell

A bump on a bony part of your body, such as your shin or head, can cause a lump. Your skin swells because there is less room underneath for the blood to drain away.

A blood clot becomes a scab which protects the cut while it heals. Underneath, new skin cells are made to replace the damaged ones. Soon the scab dries up and falls off.

Broken bones

If a bone gets broken, your body has to make new cells to grow over the break and join the bone together again. The bone must be set (put) in the right position and kept still while it mends.

Special photographs called X-rays show where and how the bone is broken.

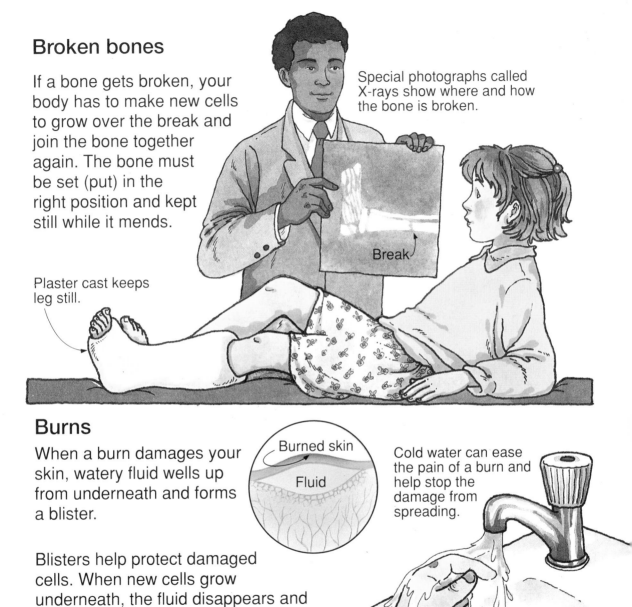

Break

Plaster cast keeps leg still.

Burns

When a burn damages your skin, watery fluid wells up from underneath and forms a blister.

Burned skin

Fluid

Cold water can ease the pain of a burn and help stop the damage from spreading.

Blisters help protect damaged cells. When new cells grow underneath, the fluid disappears and the old, damaged skin peels away.

17

Going to the doctor

Sometimes you may need help from a doctor to get better. A doctor's job is to recognize an illness and try to put things right.

Finding out what's wrong

The doctor asks you questions about how you are feeling. If you can describe your symptoms clearly, it helps her to tell what is wrong. She also looks and feels for any signs of illness such as a rash or swelling.

The doctor may feel your neck. If the lymph nodes there are swollen, it shows you have an infection.

She may put a thermometer under your tongue to take your temperature. It should be about 37°C (98.4°F).

A stethoscope makes sounds inside you louder so she can check that your heart and lungs are working properly.

Records of your health and past visits give the doctor clues to what is wrong.

She uses a special light to look inside your ears, throat and eyes.

When a doctor is working out what is wrong with you, it is called making a diagnosis. Once she has done this, the doctor can then give you advice about getting better.

Hospital

Occasionally your doctor may decide to send you to a hospital. Here you can see another doctor who knows all about your particular illness. In different parts of a hospital doctors treat different illnesses.

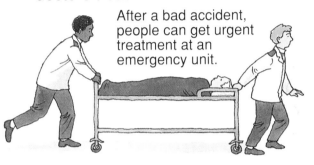

After a bad accident, people can get urgent treatment at an emergency unit.

If you have to stay in a hospital for a while, nurses will look after you. A close member of your family may be able to stay with you and friends can visit to cheer you up.

Medicine

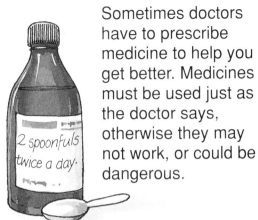

2 spoonfuls twice a day.

Sometimes doctors have to prescribe medicine to help you get better. Medicines must be used just as the doctor says, otherwise they may not work, or could be dangerous.

Doctors on the move

In parts of the world far from towns, people cannot easily get to a doctor so doctors travel to see them. They stay a short while in each place to give people treatment, and advice about staying healthy.

19

Where you live

People's health is affected by where they live, what they do and how much money they have. Different illnesses are found in different parts of the world.

Weather

The weather can affect people's health. For instance, in hot, wet parts of the world, mosquitoes can spread a serious disease called malaria.

Mosquitoes can infect people with malaria when they bite them.

Food

In some poorer parts of the world, there is not always enough food to go around. Without all the goodness they need from food, people can get very ill. This is called malnutrition.

Red areas on this map show poorer parts of the world.

AFRICA

Not all food is good for you. In richer parts of the world many people suffer from diseases which doctors think may be caused by eating too much of the wrong kind of food.

This meal has lots of sugar and fat, which is bad for you.

In parts of Africa, many people die every year from malnutrition.

20

Pollution

Pollution can harm all living things, including people. For instance, polluted lakes and rivers can make people ill if the water gets into their drinking supplies.

Overcrowding

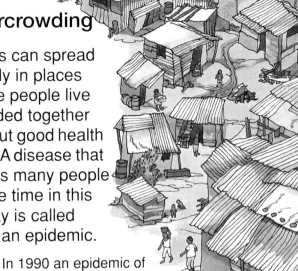

Illness can spread quickly in places where people live crowded together without good health care. A disease that infects many people at one time in this way is called an epidemic.

In 1990 an epidemic of cholera in South America affected many people who lived in poor places like the one in this picture.

Jobs

The places where people work, and the jobs they do, can affect their health.

People who work down mines can suffer breathing problems from the dust.

Knowing the facts

Learning about how your body works and how illnesses happen helps you live a healthier life.

Years ago nobody knew that smoking caused serious heart and lung diseases. Now people can learn to stay healthier by not smoking.

21

Staying healthy

There are lots of things you can do to help you stay healthy. These are some of them.

Eating well

You need to eat many different types of food to stay really healthy. How much you eat is important too. Eating too much or too little can be unhealthy.

Foods like rice, pasta and potatoes give you energy.

Meat, chicken and fish help you grow.

Dairy products such as cheese make your bones and teeth grow strong.

Fruit and vegetables contain vitamins which keep your body working well.

Keeping yourself clean

Keeping your body clean can help stop germs from causing infections.

Washing and brushing your hair helps keep headlice away.

Brushing your teeth regularly helps prevent tooth decay. Tiny pieces of food that stick in your mouth can produce acids which rot your teeth.

Cleaning your fingernails gets rid of any dirt that might carry germs.

Cuts and grazes should be washed and kept protected.

Washing your hands after going to the toilet or before eating helps stop many germs from spreading.

PASTA

Being careful

You can avoid many accidents and injuries by being careful of things that can harm you.

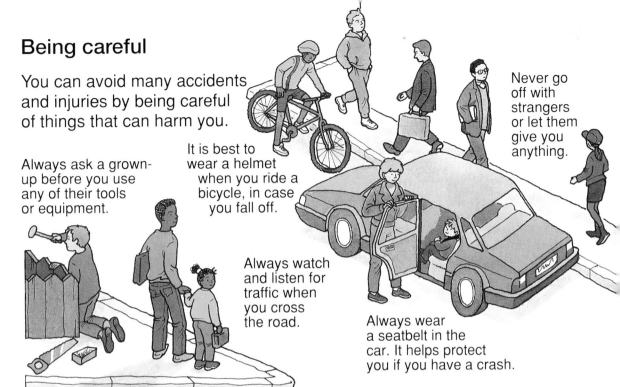

Never go off with strangers or let them give you anything.

Always ask a grown-up before you use any of their tools or equipment.

It is best to wear a helmet when you ride a bicycle, in case you fall off.

Always watch and listen for traffic when you cross the road.

Always wear a seatbelt in the car. It helps protect you if you have a crash.

Exercise

Exercising is a good way of looking after your body. It keeps it in good working order and helps prevent illness.

Swimming is good for people with asthma because it helps improve their breathing.

Feeling good

If ever you feel worried or upset, it can help to talk to somebody you know well and trust. Your friends and family can often make you feel better. Having friends and feeling loved is good for everybody's health.

23

Index

First published in 1993 by Usborne Publishing Ltd, 83-85 Saffron Hill, London EC1N 8RT, England. Copyright © 1993 Usborne Publishing Ltd. First published in America August 1993.